In these poems, Jessica Mookherjee inhabits several identities in her 'bone-framed coat'. With overarching themes of migration, otherness, sexual awakening, maternal mental illness, the impact of catastrophe, of loss and being lost, *Flood* is a debut collection from a genuine virtuoso with a powerful original voice.

Jessica Mookherjee is of Bengali heritage and grew up in South Wales. Her poetry has been widely published in journals, and in two pamphlets, *The Swell* (Telltale Press, 2016) and *Joyride* (The Black Light Engine Room Press, 2017). She was highly commended in the Forward Prize 2017 for best single poem. Jessica works in Public Health and lives in Kent. Flood is her first full collection.

The language of Jessica Mookherjee's poems is vividly immediate, with its own rich culture, distinctive rhythms and striking imagery. The separate stories in the poems of *Flood* flow together into a single current, deep and powerful enough to evoke the experience of several lives.

Susan Wicks, author of *De-iced* and *House of Tongues*

Jessica Mookherjee's *Flood* is an at-times overwhelming read. It is dense with the loss and longing of mothers, daughters and childless women who are nevertheless also both. This tremendously unified book demands to be read at a single sitting, and is a striking testament to a life lived – and survived.

Fiona Sampson MBE, author of *On the White Plain: the search for Mary Shelley*, and *Limestone Country*

In this collection Jessica Mookeherjee is a genuine virtuoso with a powerful original voice. She creates a vivid cosmos as, with verve, she cuts through façades, plunges into depths and shows a gutsy life on the edge of things. Wales, England, London, Bengal, India and elsewhere are woven with wondrous imagination and sharp, incisive imagery into the poems, all of which breathe and flow with a music all her own, exposing what it is to live and be brought up in our multi-cultural society. This is poetry worth noting.

Patricia McCarthy, editor of Agenda (www.agendapoetry.co.uk)

Also by Jessica Mookherjee

The Swell (Telltale Press, 2016)
Joyride (The Black Light Engine Room Press, 2017)

For my mother,
Bichitra Devi
with love

to Niel,

FLOOD

Jessica Mookherjee

Much Love Jess xx

Cultured Llama Publishing

First published in 2018 by
Cultured Llama Publishing
www.culturedllama.co.uk

A CIP record for this book is available from The British Library

ISBN 978-0-9957381-1-9

Printed in Great Britain by Lightning Source UK Ltd

Cover design: Mark Holihan

Photographer: Steve Collins

Contents

ii. Flow

iii. Break

iv. Surge

i. Churn

The Flesh Leaves

A road, paths, and a series of moments,
shaking hands, you tell me you're dying,
that you'd never again remember this...

being one thing after another, as flesh leaves,
I exist one second to the next. You speak
about a limpet dislodged from a rock.

Caught on a fierce wave – saw such visions,
then returned by the flood, others called him Messiah.
You're covered in leaves, on a cliff's edge,

with a tree's memory, asking where chaos
comes from. *A phone call, a cigarette, hunger,*
thirst, a promise. I don't keep love letters...

You say leaves don't keep you warm.
Can you face where you are going? You smile,
say we'll jump holding hands ... into the sea.

It can end anywhere, I think of holloways,
green lanes, ancient walk ways, *travel slowly,*
call me, I mean it. We made a deal.

1967

Here is a girl out of place. Stranger
and strangeness, both cold and grey.
Her sari billows in English winds, a pale,
princess clutching her wedding gold.

Red lips and bride-mark like a wound
on her head, she walks behind him.
She walks away from here, away from
her mother, father – who gave her to him.

How quickly the shame sets in.
Feeling dirty under clean British sheets.
Alone and out of time as her bleeding stops
and her first child starts to kick.

Small

I called you minnow, in those shambles of afterbirth,
where I was splayed in mad shame.

I made rainbows from oil-slicked pools on the hospital
floor. I should know your name in this room

where I am struck dumb with these smells
of haemorrhage. I name you snow, woebegone.

They dressed you in white, put you in my arms.
My breath is too short to call out your name.

The Milk

My Bengali mother had no idea why I wore a daffodil.
So the ladies fed me welshcakes
and told me why I wore a black hat on St David's Day.
Dewi Sant, I wasn't sure
who he was, but I thought I heard him in the waves
off the Mumbles head.
I had no grandmothers here, just the mamgus* on the bus.
Those crinkled Bridgets
were my wet-nurses, feeding me chewing gum,

peppermints and their native tongue.
Those old ladies fed me stories of frost covered forests
and Bendigeidfran.**
They were my milk. *It's comin' in, see* they said –
with an eye on the wind,
come and pray with us ... I went to their chapel, where the
wood is worshiped
and where they had me believe that the desert Bible lands
were in the mountains of North Wales.

*Mamgu is Welsh for Grandmother, ** Bendigeidfran is a giant from Welsh myth.

Glass Sisters

Kuan-Yin was locked in a glass case
for most of the seventies and eighties.
She is still there, almost forgotten
next to other relics, pottery, from Bangladesh.

We were all cabinet curios,
waking occasionally, trapped behind glass,
under small locks, tiny keys.
Gingerly, with a smell of fresh rose-water

she would take us out, sit us on the sofa,
while she played with a typewriter,
practising her name. No-one but us
saw her hair unbraided,

cascades of shining black.
Her fingers spelling, yours sincerely,
clicking on the white Olympus –
I could get a job, learn to drive, drink wine

she muttered, glancing at her dolls.
I looked sideways at Kuan-Yin
behind her pane; she smiled at me
and listened to the world's sorrows.

The Fish Curry

He grew things from seed. They came
in boxes – little tiny sprouting coffins,
green tips and the smell of rot.
That year he got a bumper crop.
The good, dark soil kept giving him
onion after onion.
An army of small bald babies,
he lay them on the lawn to dry –
under the over-grinning sky that soon filled
with a million crying herring-gulls.

In the kitchen she gutted fish, cutting
flesh, raw, removing grey sacs, black veins
with a rutting knife, and the stench
of blood filling the house
and falling
through the drains. Occasionally
in the heat – she patted her belly
to check everything was still in place,
and all I recall was the buzz of a swarm
of a million flies at the window panes.

Broken Bones, Ruins and Texts*

When the three worlds were in darkness, Vishnu slept.
It was wet weather, soaked in alluvium, I was running,
    I slipped.

In the middle of the cosmic ocean, a lotus grew
In the wet, I knew my ankle would give way, an old injury
    calling

Out of his navel. Brahma came to him and said
'Go slowly, go slowly, I don't want you to break your leg.

Tell me, who you are?' Vishnu replied, 'I am the creator
Falling, and sit in an hospital, injured and fearful

Of the universe. All the worlds, and you are inside me'.
So I watched my step, but still lost the centre of my gravity.

'And who are you?' Brahma replied. 'I am self created,
And slid in quagged soil, fibula snapped, ligaments, sinew.

Everything is inside me'. Vishnu entered Brahma's mouth and saw
I was disjointed and bleating, left in sodden earth, while

All three worlds were in his belly. Astonished, he came out of
    Brahma's mouth
waiting for some help, some man in a white coat.

And said 'Now you must enter my belly and see the worlds'.
He spoke another language; in the hospital he avoided my
    mother's panic,

*Italic Line Text from: Vishnu and Brahma Create Each Other – *Kurma Purana*
(500–800 CE)

7

And so Brahma entered Vishnu's belly and saw all the worlds.
Wrapped me in wet plaster, bandaged, and set me in a
     white cast.

Then, since Vishnu had shut all the openings, Brahma came out
I could hardly bear my own weight, I was hobbled, cleft,

Of Vishnu's navel and rested on the lotus…
So my mother, triumphant, was bound to look after me.

The English Girl

An old woman grabs my hair,
calls me *memsahib*, forces rice
into my mouth with dark hands,
says I'm not in England now.

I glare, curse her, correct her.
My lips flare, mother chides me
in her soft voice, and I dream
my grandmother is a wild woman.

Grandmother calls me bastard,
my father's child, black demon.
But I'm blue as snow bubbles
at Gangotri glacier, rippled, turned

from ice to sky blue water, running,
raging at any stem of flow, singing
so loudly the sky holds its ears.
I am blue as Krishna. I run

into neighbours' houses like rain,
pool into arms of street kids, muddle
up tongues, teach them to sing in mock
English *At, Bat, Cat,* rub our heads

until I crawl with their lice.
Grandmother screams, calls me filth,
sits me between her legs, chops my locks
with rough scissors, says my mother
has made me British.

Hunger

The woodcutter, watching in the distance,
her small limbs, lank hair.
He looks sideways,
hand trembling on the axe.

There's a wave of red silk in the breeze
as she disappears,
inside his belly, deep in the gut,
he saws, he cuts, he chops.

The Child

We walk together and she takes
my big hairy hand, almost pulls me
into the woods to find wild ponies.
I steer her gently onto the common,
the high ground where wind
shakes our hair and sounds like her laughter.
Her red coat is tight around her arms,
zipped up. She asks me about seagulls,
why do they cry like that?
I tell her that they are ghosts
of dead children looking for their mothers.
Her face is a perfect circle as she takes
it in, becoming a story, she might
tell her friends. *Am I your best friend?*
She asks me, I smile, remembering the boys
at the pond so many years ago, when
we tied string to the tails of dragonflies
and flew them like kites.
Yes, my only friend. My heart stops
as she kisses the back of my hand.
We fall silent as horses appear,
watching us, from folds in the trees.

The Demographer

Uncertain what happened the next day,
the day after there was no one there
at the school gates. Unsure,
how far or close her home was,
the usual shape of her mother's sari, broken –

she waited in an ebb and flow,
unclear, watching other mothers
scoop their brood into themselves,
inside their milk-yellow smiles.
She knew, from school-books, kids her age

once worked down mines. She set off
in those brown school shoes,
up the hill, a small mountaineer, ignoring
sympathetic half concerns that murmured why
anyone would leave their baby on the road.

She felt it was the next day, after the doctors left,
that she knew they were too much for her to hold.
It was the next day she told the dinner lady
who held her hand at lunch-break,
there were too many children in the world.

Goat-Father

There is no goat-god, he told me as I sat munching
on *The Sunday Times* colour supplements,
thinking later I might trim the grass; for now
I was digesting an article on animal sacrifice in India
and frankly, it made my stomach churn.
Well what about Pan? I said, taking a leap.
He was never a man to ruminate,
and he thumped the coffee table with his fist,
barked, *Jesus Christ kid, what's got into you? There are only
elephants, tigers and monkey gods, noble beasts…*
I took a gamble, told him I was leaving the room,
depositing pellets as I left.

Scars

He was out of his skull when he said
Let's be lovers, licked my cheek like
sea-lapping the shore. He walked me
home from school

down that secret path past the cliffs
where no one was supposed to go.
He pulled me inside a cave shaped like a fist,
and gave me my first cigarette.

His eyes were like teeth,
said we should elope, steal a car,
run away to Porthcawl, and I took my first
drag as the chemical taste bit, and

he watched as I retched, said
it's a skill, and held my hair back
as I spat in the rock-pool.
He blew smoke rings as I choked.

As I heard gulls screaming
like children, I shivered,
I saw waves sneak in through
the cracks and fissures.

I don't know why I giggled
when he told me men brought girls here,
and we kissed as I touched
scars carved on the cave wall.

Dawn Chorus

He saw me in a late night shop
buying Marlborough Lights.
I only remember his beard – nothing else,
I didn't think about how he looked
at me.
He asked me out for dinner –
what went through my mind was did I look
like I needed feeding
or just like someone who'd say yes
to a chicken dinner?
I didn't know then
that to all men
a seventeen-year-old girl is beautiful –
with her ample flesh, shocked purple hair
and art school clothes.
I can't remember a single thing about him,
just the taste of the chicken fricassee,
the cushions of the limousine and the dawn chorus,
before light
as he drove me home.

Hungry Ghosts

She tries to cut her blubber, maddened
by a crazy smell of blood.
The ghosts sit still inside her, getting fattened.

On the streets, men pinch her, call her slattern.
To them her round face looks like food.
She tries to cut her blubber, maddened

inside long corridors where injections sadden.
Everything they give her does her good.
The ghosts sit still inside her, getting fattened.

They pretend to rub her belly, unenlightened
by the rude taste of her moods.
She tries to cut her blubber, maddened

and looking for the knife she wished they hadn't
used to slit her grief in two.
The ghosts sit still inside her, getting fattened.

The men count dimples on her buttocks, flatten
her hefty breasts all smeared with mud.
She tries to cut her blubber. Maddened,
the ghosts sit still inside her, getting fattened.

ii. Flow

Named

A forgotten name on the tip of his tongue,
tangled roots cough into a knot
of cries that bud into an orphan mourning.
He clings inside her belly, jostled
by sideways looks and pursed lips. Still there.

In formation, a correction of wanton
girls, hand in hand, bud out of coarse
uniforms. Tight belly, bunged inside –
he drinks her blush, grows a voice,
ears that listen for his name in muffled chords.

She won't give him up, but can't
let him drink from her. He's always still
in the next room with the nuns, an exhibition
of babies, all fattened up with starch, waiting
to fill up someone else's empty space.

Desert Gods

i. Snake

A slither made of sand, the wind cuts into cracks. Crevices turn
knife, then snakeskin, he takes a bow and arrow,

kills a sand viper, skins it alive, roasts it in grit and pity,
and all around is the adhan, calling across the Tannoy, a call to
prayer.

Sandstorm cuts into needles slipping through pores of skin.
It whips like a cat-o-nine tails. All the hotel staff have gone,

his parents in bed. The boy waits for the storm to grind him
into sand, blow him away. His stepfather sells

him snake-oil, grins like desert wind – he must learn what
fear is.
What's normal about this? He feels the snake of wind

tighten as the oil refinery burns. The desert sun smiles
too brightly, like a man making a deal, knows he's duped you,

works for the oil company, *and all around is the adhan,*
calling across the Tannoy, the boy can't hear words blown
by wind,

all because he's someone else's, has to learn what fear is.
His stepfather tells him to be a man, whatever that is.

The refinery burns, *call me Dad,* an empty hotel, *and all around*
is the adhan, calling across the Tannoy, a call to prayer.

The boy's locked out, knows behind closed doors
his mother can kiss, and he's ready to face snakes in the heat,

mistakes the call to prayer for something obscene, screams out
to let him in, *and all around is the adhan and the snake's hiss.*

ii. Scorpion
Scrape and craw, nail scratch on door, black metal
from heat parch. She could use a new helmet, a slew

of armour made like lead *and all around is the adhan, over
the Tannoy,*
believe in peace. She's imperfect, made from god's spit,

waddles, clanking, blackened from place to place.
She'll learn shame – it's decreed, *and all around is the adhan,*

over the Tannoy, come to success. She won't get into shape,
won't fit,
wears bone over flesh, learns how to kill with a sting.

She grows hard, freezes in desert night, watches them kiss,
and the muezzin calls in favours, writes lists

of all God's wishes, *and all around is the adhan, over the Tannoy,*
God is great. She'll learn the shame that her brother can't,

raise armies of scorpions and crayfish.
They march while her mother and stepfather kiss

with the lights on, *and all around is the adhan, over the Tannoy,*
above her sobbing, they hang soiled sheets from a window.

See what you've done now? Exoskeleton and poison,
You didn't save me. Her brother finds her hiding,

she tells him *make the best of it,* sweating and shiny,
scuttling and fierce. She strikes hate from her nature,

waits for wounded men, stings them with love.
There's no shame in hate that looks like self defence,

*and all around is the adhan, over the Tannoy, come to the one
who is blest, come to heaven, come to prayer,* rise from the flames.

iii. The Lizard
Palm trees, cop show cars, wide open roads, men in robes
flank the oil refinery burning in the distance. His mother kisses

a man who's not his father. *Domestic bliss,* whispers his sister,
*and all around is the adhan, over the Tannoy, come to prayer,
    white boy,*

learn what fear is. God's a desert. His mother looks past him,
needs to know what love is, goes back to the house, bright lit

windows, takes off her dress, *and all around is the adhan, over
the Tannoy, come to prayer.* Listen to god in the wind.

His mother won't hold him, points to hot sand, says
that's where she'll go, covered in dust to burn in petrol.

The boy walks into sun-blasted desert to find something
to kill with a knife, sticks and dynamite, *and all around*

is the adhan, over the Tannoy, come to prayer, find God in your hand.
He swears he'll call no one father, stays in the desert,

sits in a circle, still before sunset, parched and poised
to catch her. She arrives dressed like a salamander,

he can't hold her or the desert inside him, he hums
with the muezzin, *and all around is the adhan, over the Tannoy,*

come to prayer, find love in crevices. The lizard jugs towards him,
he stabs with a pocket knife, burns her with petrol.

She bleeds. Feeds him and offers him peace, whispers
in hiss language, in scuttle tongue survival, *stay alive, child,*

she drops her ticking twitch of tail in his hand, runs back
    to hell.
and all around is the adhan, over the Tannoy, come to prayer,

notice your will to live in a desert. He watches the lizard taste
his scent sly from the hard place, he becomes her escape.

The Walkabout

Inside I was dried, lichen growing between my heart-valves,
nothing was a map.

Outside I stood in wet verges, followed winding lanes
outside the village

There was a sign: *Disappointment Welcomes
Careful Drivers,*

and as my bone-framed coat carried me to the edge,
I looked back.

I'd thought it said Hollywood – or just a place I would be
welcomed with lights.

Neither young nor old, I scattered in brambles and moss.
I was soaked in fine mist,

I was mildew and mould. She stopped as I waved
a thumb into the unknown.

A signal I'd learned. Inside the car, life was like a sparrow flown
into a stranger's kitchen.

I thought I was crying, wailing *take me home … with you …
please…*

Instead we talked about the weather, the Dales, and being
sixteen.

She held my hand just a little too long as she let me down
at the junction on the A66.

Green Tara

I will find her, twisting on the steps
as she drops her head, zig-zags her way
to Sunday school. I'll have no idea
who she is at first, then why not … why yes …
I'll be heavy with beads and bangles, wear
hearts coloured on my cheek and hair
shocked and pink, meandering
in Oxfam Vivienne Westwood down
Marylebone High Street, bigger than the world.
I'll watch for her, full every night, praying,
burning upwards to my dipped eyes.
She'll turn up for supper, thinking this and that,
looking for me, looking for someone slim and white.
I will send her trees to take care of her,
I will turn her mother normal,
I will watch her tell her first lie,
I will wish for her to be a child, just that,
a child in a green pullover wishing
her to dream of me in red silk dress.
We'll glimpse each other through branches
as together we'll change everything.

Wildlife

Half-Asleep Roger sold them marijuana in the yard.
She and Wide-Awake Dave sat up all night, shaved
ends off blotting paper. They cast them like I-Ching.
He told her she was a shape-shifter like him.

She smelled his burning van on the Latimer Road
the night the gangstas fired the yard.
In the morning they threw flowers into his charred
remains. She became an owl that day.

Half-Asleep sat with her all night,
because she thought the sky would fall on her head,
wore a crash helmet to keep her safe. They lit joints
on the smouldering ashes of their friend.

Half-Asleep gave her Wide-Awake Dave's
left over papers, *you know what to do with these* he said.
She shuffled them like tarot cards. *You can tell the future
with them* Wide-Awake Dave whispered from his grave.

She became a doe, gradually, as tiny pin-pricks of light
grabbed her throat and the moon punched her outside
Manor House tube, and she saw stars falling into life.
She ran inside Finsbury Park, to feel safe, like prey.

During the day, she followed magpies in Epping Forrest.
Twig-trails and ivy flickering on raw bark; the birds told her
she was a fox. She hid inside a woman's flesh, put make up on,
clutched her season ticket, wide-awake, ready to bite.

Growing Up in Nightclubs

Kurt Cobain won't grow old; his bleak words smash
    my faith in songs.
My lovers are carefully grown to repeat mistakes
    over and over…
My mother writes every week, tells me she won't leave
    that bastard,
I just groan and throw away her letters.

My lovers are carefully grown to repeat these mistakes
    over and over…
My mother says she has no room to invite me home
    for Christmas.
I just groan and throw away her letters
and I just keep yelling *Look at me, look at me*.

My mother says she has no room to invite me home
    for Christmas.
My soap-bubble friends glint pretty in light, in cold
    ice nightclubs
and I just keep yelling *Look at me, look at me*,
and they leave stains on me like rust-marks in a bathtub.

My soap-bubble friends glint pretty in light. In cold
    ice nightclubs
Kurt Cobain won't grow old; his bleak words smash
    my faith in songs
and they leave stains on me like rust-marks in a bathtub.
My mother writes every week, tells me she won't leave
    that bastard.

Taliesin

Once there was a boy made of amber,
inside him was a trapped fly.
He was the moon's frozen light with
long silver fingers and songs that charmed
juice from girls' thighs. He forgot that
he'd swallowed a fly. Perhaps he died
in a North London room made of blotting paper.

He'd sing in the language of birds,
named thousands of stars, and found
their lonely dark places in the eyes of a girl
that he met in a flat off Holloway Road,
carrying the other half of his madness. In a fury
of whirling, she churned heat to let blood flow,
resin melt in three drops. Perhaps they died together.

She swallowed a fly as he kissed her.
Perhaps she died in a room made of amber.
She became a spider and span a web as far
as the universe would let her, bound them together,
then handed him scissors to cut himself free.
Instead he fashioned the moon from blotting paper,
swallowed it, and wrote sad songs about her.

Full Moon Over Finsbury Park

Bathed in sheen, Finsbury Park disappears
in moonlight. We ask a woman made of night,
where we are, she draws a map on a pack of cigarettes,
points to the gap in a fence, says she won't kiss us
because she's shaped like an owl, and we leave
to the music of hooting and panting in your head.

Across railway lines, in the pub, a fat man on the sign,
we play a game of demonic pool, drunk. The balls
spin like satellites as we talk about gravity.
We're still lost as we leave, I smash my glass
on the pavement. You, locked into your myths of blood,
shipyards, mud flats. I – in all the seas of the moon,

of nectar, alone and struck by the dares you set me,
not fully pushed out yet, holding onto your hand
in the seas known as vapours, clouds, islands.
I pick some honesty from the dark places of the park
and put them in my bag. You pick flowers by moonlight,
laugh and hold me tight as we find our way home.

House on Fire

Is this how we left him – in that burning house? We didn't dare
mock, as he impressed the birds on the roof top,
told me he was Quetzalcoatl, pointed out how
    many edges existed in the house.

You played him mantras, sang me songs.
Let's go for a walk, you said, in the middle of the night.
Let's take in the air, I'll show you all the best places, a car park

on the estate rooftop can be Hotel California, this park bench,
near the housing office, this is Central Park. You told me
    your dreams
about the sky, golden leaves, and being everywhere at once.

Let's sit here, you said, suddenly shy, on the other side
    of the world.
We held hands for a hundred years. I wanted to write
our names in indelible ink as we burned a future into us,
    that night.

We've left him behind in the burning house, I whispered, and you
became the bitten dark as the rain came gently
surrounding us, a mist of yellow street light,
    a bathing wash of gold leaves.

Was this where we left each other, on a park bench,
on the Harvest Estate? I turned my face away from midnight,
just for a second, said your name. I was scared of the love

you had in your hand, I fled, said *let's pretend*
    we're Hollywood stars, or in New York,
or somewhere else. You held me for a moment, replied,
Let's go back, it's late, and our friend's alone in a house on fire.

This was how we left him, fighting feathered serpents,
police men surrounding him, in handcuffs.
Did my mantras madden him?
You said, as we walked hand in hand to the World's End,

where we sat on the swings, no homeland, no diamonds,
no escape, in a small disintegration of land, all burnt down,
we were together, covered in leaves, covered in feathers.

Floriography

i. Agapanthus

Our love flowered in a summer, died with grandparents,
  grew transcendent.
Open to what we could pour in, cold, moss, dampness,
  bitter herbs, ethanol, dynamite. Mouths open,
  our hands like trees clawing at sky. You had things to do,
I suspected. I was tending the dead.
  When summer returned we were quite changed.

ii. Dill

Arriving, red hot borsht, cold soup and sour cream.
  Leaving, fermented.
I say – *go and see a doctor, check everything,*
  get tested for diabetes, inflammation.
I won't do it. I'll travel to Poland on an overnight train,
listen to Bob Dylan on headphones
  eat Mizeria with hard boiled eggs.

iii. Forget-Me-Not

We stood in scorpion grass, a field of bullet mud
  somewhere in Somerset, listening to a band.
We saw five hundred species of human
  humming to the music, I can't remember anything.
You were shot with a fire of root systems that germinated
  inside you.
I was small and probably thinking I would forget this
  moment.

iv. Sweet Pea

Like Odysseus, we have all been seduced
  by the wrong drugs in our wine,
slept with the wrong people, blown by winds
in the wrong direction, and somehow found our way back
  home.

On our return we find our genes mutated and poisoned,
but our colours and stories – intensified.

v. Pink Carnation

I'm all yours in this budding place. I have flowers opening
    all over my skin,
my internal organs bloom. No one cries petals like I do.
You wave a rose like a red flag and I'm kissing your eyes,
which have turned away. I will keep them
    safe in my pocket.

The Jezebel Spirit

I'll build a swimming pool on the moon and fill
it full of rocket fuel. I'll burn inside my breast strokes
while breathing fire. Each afternoon, I'll build a potting shed
with roses climbing through black holes. I'll mend
windows in my luxury lunar home, learn how to wire
in the electrics, plug in loud speakers,
    and boom out celestial music.

But, I'm nowhere near the orbit, light years from midnight
stars. With no spacecraft or screwdrivers, only pockets
full of flat batteries, a crooked sixpence someone flung at me,
an absinthe spoon and sugar cubes. I can't reach myself
with these implements, only pull out my guts
and abandon them. I've lost the spit of my loneliness,
    stuffed them into acorns and buried them.

In a thrust of soil, I want to sleep inside a grave
made of flowers gathered by a bower bird,
to quiet my engines, become the exhale of a planet.
I want to see loud beauty in the thrall of trees, melt into
air that can't be breathed by people who are not there,
and disappear into the bright furnace
    that exists inside the big sky.

The Father
for Simon

I'm struck blue, bottle-green wings unfolding
on a sunlit window – I think of her, those years,

child-still, pushing wooden shapes into holes,
and in my silence I keep the quiet going.

In the park pond, before floods, she yells –
the paddle boat's peddling her, my arm round her.

And later, in the pool, her water-wings can't help,
so I hold her. It is so quiet. She must remember

my shape. The sound of my voice singing to her,
don't worry, every little thing gonna be alright…

Now outside, I watch the river bend like a girl,
unfurl in the curl of her dance as she curses rain.

I think she pulls wings from blue-bottles,
punches them into a sky filled with fathers, and flies away.

The River God's Daughter

His daughter asks him what river-water tastes like
in hell, and he foams from his lips –
sings *Mahandi, Godavari, Hugli.*

Downstream, near the bank, a mix of fresh water
and salt where the merge occurs, in drift
of moon-spit, all washed up.

He never thought he would have daughters,
never thought a spell would turn him
into Shylock, Indra, Lear –

he never taught them to swim. Her sister sneers
When rivers die they are reborn as weather.
Better burn him at the estuary.

He names her Padma, Lotus, Flood, pulls on her hair
as she looks for a husband in the the pull of tides,
but there is too much weather,

sailors blown into thunder, before the river inhales,
cries and spits them into mountains, and drops
his daughter into the cracks of earth

as he collects in clouds – looking for sons, and the girl
keeps running, as he hisses of fat
on the estuary bank, she keeps running,

in tributaries, meanders, rises from her bed, churns,
gets up for work, keeps going, keeps running,
keeps running to the sea.

iii. Break

The River Man

Hard water, you curl soft-lapping
slaps against your green tide-marked chest.
Roman nose, flared, you turn cheek bones,

your receding hair-line to the sea, out to Tilbury.
You knew what the rush of wind would bring.
Your knotted brows saw the tea-clipper off

with sea shanties and rum. Fish swam in your cataract
eyes and your cracked breast.
Boatmen barged stones on your back. You forget

once you were the tideway, Tamas,
the dark man, the slither – pushing into yourself,
into a land denned by banks, planks, turnpikes and sewers.

Your tide turns to the sound of bells, gulls,
applause and mobile phone ring tones.
You still have that dirty tongue and a strong-man swell.

Red

The red curtains in my mother's house
looked like blood dripping down
the windows. The red tika on my mother's
forehead looked like someone had shot her.
When I first wore red lipstick, smacked
across my face, she said it was inappropriate
for a girl of six, *wash it off,* she said.
When I first wore that red silk skirt
it mesmerised me by the way it moved
around my legs. It made you smile at me.
Now your face is red, too much sun,
too much beer, too much butter. I tell you
not to wear that red shirt. This month,
there's blood in the bathroom again.

Fossil Record

On the beach, you remarked on my height,
You're a different species. We kissed under big sky
and compared our foreheads,
I, Neanderthal, you said proudly,
you, Afarensis.
Your face was full of the sea,
you grabbed a rock and threw it as far as you could.

In Hadar, that ape-faced Lucy
reached out of the sand,
walked out of rock, into the arms of a man.
Tiny, she danced out of the East African Rift
to the Beatles playing on a radio, making it
into the future. In Ethiopia they call her Dinkinesh,
means *You're Marvellous.*

I followed your big footsteps on Brancaster Beach, imagined
slipping on the saltpools of Afar.
You said *Let's walk across the North Sea together.*
I let you place your man-hands on my waist, you called me
Dinkinesh and handed me a piece of flint.

We are so young, you said, making sparks
as you held my hand over sand dunes,
but I only held Geological terms,
and our future.

The Lascaux Caves

Folding rock becomes
liquid, becomes solid.
It is all the same to her.
She gapes and grins
from every orifice
as they
paint her calluses and
ingrained skin.
Inside her it is hot and dank
and lit
by animal fat that
becomes her tattoos.
The never-maiden holds
her bellicose breath, then
whispers to her shaman
in gibberish, the secrets
to keep the horses running.

Shopping List

The machine's broken, the check out girl
taps the side of her head.

Unspoken, forgetting things over again,
repeating myself. Crying in a supermarket.

Lost in the freezer section, remembering
don't feel love – to spite absent gods.

Slip in spilt milk on aisle six, a voice asks,
Are you all right?

Not crying about that, just crying
as memories awake – how the machine broke.

Pacing, making things up, to you and sometimes
to strangers. If the lies are right

things might be all right, and stop,
pick up fragments in the drinks section,

in the pharmacy, and the bits hidden
in make up.

Your Lost Mother

You call her to untangle your hair,
tell you stories from the mouths of whales,

disentangle your days of office work,
listen to your list of moans and ready-meals.

She's so soft, bruised from her climb down
from the Bay of Rainbows, she comes, invisible

when you are slow-awake. You occasionally
watch for her in the jagged space outside your eyes,

as you listen to obnoxious thoughts of this
and that – all bothering hums and static hiss,

and you can smell her crazy breasts in the numb
light, taste her cold and disembodied milk.

Seder

I sat with you, Esther Drukartz,
when I bathed you in 1992.
We talked about your tattoo,
and when they turned you
into a number.
Tell me about Pesach, I asked you,
at Seder, in Kilburn.
It's the one where we have cheesecake,
you answered, and we both laughed.
Edith Metzger paces up and down.
She never sat still all the way to England,
Toni Reich's accent rasps
She called that Nazi, who pushed her mutti away
as she got on the kindertransport,
a very rude man, she was so brave.
Edith Metzger paces up and down.

Erna Kurtz, Bessie Rieterbund, Gabriel Makeler,
Johanna Ernst, Annie Weitzenfeld, Sophie Driels.

I will say your names and visit
all the places you lived.
I sit in the Musee Juif de Belgique
with a sad collection,
a fast bottom-drawer clear-out of tattered
prayer shawls, Hebrew books,
menorahs.
Friends ask, *why do you do this?*
I go from Krakow, to Tallinn,
From Riga to Berlin,
Budapest, to Antwerp to St.Petersberg.
Summoned by ghosts calling in Shabbos.

In the cab back to the hotel,
I chat with the driver, *I'm from England*
I say and he tells me he is from Rwanda.
all my family died he says.
Are you OK now? I ask, filling the flood
of space with words I cannot bare,
Of course not, he replies.

The Safe House

He asks me to stay for a weekend
in November, and I'm still watching for all signs
of him to fade.

This house is a safe mist, curdling
around the edges, a silence blocked
from change.

Couples have failed in rooms,
conceived futures with no names.
This house is thin

with sighs, a presence of awkward smiles.
Nothing can change in this house
until it's certain,

I don't want to say *yes* just yet,
and the small jade loop he gave me
when he left

still hangs on a red thread on the door hook.
I don't admit he was a kind man,
and that I was wrong.

Resting Place

I build them a rest home, all my dead friends,
from the things I find in my pockets and handbag,
silver coins for their eyelids, tiger's eye,
a crushable heart, tissues, bus tickets, torch,
maps, notebooks, an old toffee, things to entice.

I build them a place to call home, all those dead relations,
many I didn't know, grandmothers
whose names I've forgotten, aunts who died barren,
dead children who my grandmother left
outside for three days to clear their lungs of disease.
I give them big windows, easy to open, and rooms that change

size depending on their whims, for the dead are moody,
mutable things. I fill their home with candles,
a big fire to pour incense, as it's my tradition.
I call out to them in Sanskrit,
in Mongolian, in gibberish. I call them in.
At first they are skeptical, uncommitted,

notice the dust, shake the windows, but soon they laugh.
Their laughter sounds like rainfall and footsteps.
They sit with me a while, purr, pat my shoulder,
keep me company. One aunt, I never met, strokes my hair
    and whispers,
only the living are lonely for the dead.

Having my Sister for Dinner

We try to forget over a wine that tastes of grapefruit,
and the kids next door make me anxious, with their creaking,
crying out and music too loud. They are living, I suppose.

You say things I've said that upset you. I say I never said them,
or perhaps didn't mean what I said. And you say
I don't know who I am to you.

You say, I was so big, huge, that you stopped
brushing your teeth when I left home, you don't remember
why. I want to say, *but it was so long ago*

but don't because time folds us into origami boats
made by praying fools. I want to pull you from my spleen
and spit you back into your soul.

Rosetta Stone

Rosetta writes the wrongs, upside down,
scratches onion ink into her cheeks,
collects the tears in the sink, drains them
into songs and photographs of bones.

She doesn't go out into the world,
with its disorganised streets,
waits instead in her room of glyphs,
next to flesh as her only friend.

She can't tell so many things, her throat
can't swallow the silence. Her aqueducts
are all cut up, the fire escape blocked by bins.
She's always cold like an Antarctic wind.

Her flesh offers to warm her hands, she thinks
there will be nothing left but the codes
if she disappears in the heat. So she rights
herself inside a whirlwind, her hair

looking backcombed and interesting,
she grins at the night as her tears and milk
dry, and thinks she might save embers,
keep memories alive

in her pocket, write all the wrongs she did
out a hundred times in letters of guilt
and only fire and wind survive
to understand her translations.

Astrology

Jupiter has undone me
with his love of chaos,
horologists will rip up clocks
into conjunctions and tatters.

I stood with my blood
at the meridian, watching light
bounce from Thames to tea clipper.
At the last transit, a leaf fell

into my hand, in a tight spiral.
On that spot, I watched it twist
in night gusts, yearning for soil.
Have I turned this life

after the chaos, moving from postcode
to postcode, my make up too heavy
like Jupiter? I bulldozed everything
out of my path, before resting

to colder positions, paying tax,
taking more baths,
learning to drive,
taking out insurance.

Yew

Stripped and stabbed,
pierced with growing fingernails
turned into wood, after years
of lying covered in green flesh. All holes in you,
relentless in sucks and blows, on and on.
Fires elf-shot into you to the sound of peeling.
The world is ants, mites and funerary rites,
the scurrying sound of disintegration
burns copper green, saved for winter,
from heartache, a namesake.

In Case

A small book on mushrooms, field guide
to foraging; in case of remaining hope,
walking boots and gloves.
A flint fire-stick, a box of tinder,
sleeping bag and tarp.
A case of fish-hooks and twine,
pen-knife well sharpened – in case of love.

In case of emergency take also
fifty-thousand seeds placed inside
bio-hazard proof canisters – warning:
keep dry, minimum moisture ten percent.
Take also – just in case, ninety-five tons of earth
turned and mulched by a million worms,
take enough water, take bees.

A book of knock-knock jokes,
a pen, in case of inspiration, ink made from leaves,
an A to Z to navigate the burning streets,
and some pillows – in case of exhaustion.
I will make us a cosy fire to warm our feet,
laugh at stupid gags and the way it ends
as we drink fly agaric tea.

Naming Things

There was a famous naturalist who,
returning from South America, told

how every time he looked he found
a new species of moss, beetle, flower.

He said it must be how God felt,
I name you this, and this and this.

As I stroll up the banks of this
English hill, and pass well trodden,

manicured paths lined with plants
whose names I never learned,

I find a Rhododendron tree,
hold my breath and climb inside.

Stroking it's sharp-tipped leaves,
I ask what it's name really is;

it laughs in sounds heard only by bees,
and whispers it. If you utter

true names of plants you will stay
forever at that place. Your mouth

will turn to fibrous bark,
and your eyes will fill with knots and birds.

Your hair will rustle in the wind, alive
with leaves and creeping woody things.

Love Spells

Standing in an in between, somewhere people sang
and walked in circles. It's a ruin now, graffiti
carved walls and scars, and its tea time,
and I'm in a band of travellers. This happens to me
sometimes. I look for where I must make a magic,
then those people come, they come and tell me
the same things they always tell me. That I am wine
but not like wine, funny, but only the first time.
I have everything I need to make the spell good,
I have young flesh, girls just not quite women.
Here – I show them to the sky, in the open
hand of God, let it pour me.

I imagine you, somewhere – perhaps asleep, perhaps not –
and I don't feel hungry anymore.
I'm soaking in the rain, and I imagine that you have a red
car and smart shoes and all your fingers and toes.
And the darkness is evaporated and replaced
by eyes that crease at the edges, and large, strapping
arms that hold on to the world as it ends.

Yes, I'm still there. Some place that still exists,
Last year I tried the spell again, and I threw
everything I had into the mix, I even made young girls
shout – but times have changed. The children were more
interested in iPhones than clouds trapped in jars.
I had little to interest them in my cupped hands of earth,
in a willow cabin. I called and I wonder
are you still stirring, am I calling loud enough?
Am I even calling?

The Luxury

i.

I'm perky, bouncing on the bonnet, a little brown berry,
my fat legs, not yet disappointed.

ii.

I'm no longer Ford Fiesta, I'm climbing into a cool
blue Aston Martin, feel power even in the glove compartment,
a chassis emitting a charisma of bones, all high structured,
balanced for speed. My suit of carbon, styled in luxury.
A leather bound run over anything, and purr
in tune with each design around me. Most important,
admired by men.

iii.

Unbuttoned, face down, marked. A thorn cuts
my finger, gets right in under my nail. It hurts.
It's all I'm thinking about. My poor little finger
with it's snagged nail. It's all I can think about.

iv.

Insulated, zipped in weatherproof,
I crunch the snow, run dominant in each step,
my firm tread, cold and easy inside me now. My lover
is the wind, strokes my burning cheek, I march
towards a fragile flutter of a flag that secures my stride.

v.

Suddenly, I'm running, my joints bubble.
I'm ham and hock. Suckling milk
and other proteins – I walk, light step, one foot,
ball to toe, step, ahead for miles,
flanks rest on haunch, pant then,
hoot, as I am delicious animal.

vi.

The mirror's confused. Doesn't know me, caught eyes wide.
It's suspicious, eyebrows raised. I'm unzipped, caressed
as I unroll and pamper, ooze from places unknown to maps.

iv. Surge

Before the Rut

Gauche-eyed deer dart, aproned next to lattes and flat whites, angle their long limbs, hinds iced in reflected glass, to murmurs of soft-haired women in scarves, talking in whispers, about all that naughty almond and chocolate brioche. Barely looking at those dappled daughters caught behind hissing coffee counters, invisible in bouncing light, waiting for Cernunnos.

> Counting pashminas, Cath Kidston, women in turquoise flowers, stresses in their accents camouflaged as rustling leaves, discussing soft furnishings. Unthinking, one sticks her tongue out, smelling musk. Doe-soft for her choice, servicing riding boots, Saturday sports-casual, they pray to the corn god, take wafer before the lek, his hungry advice, graze Kent's Finest Products,

> waiting for Cernunnos.

The Otherwise

No forests, cradles, no lush thickets, no tangles
of briar, thorn, no bonnets, no cries in the night,
nothing to miss, nothing to be defeated by no berries,
nothing ripe, no honey, no pull of tide in the breast.

Wide open fields to play in for life, prairie grass,
big, big sky, trees touch tip to tip and tap root,
an absence of clouds, stones, sometimes open valves,
sometimes shut, as I wish, a lost key, locked outside.

Bau*

Fur guarded, with down-hair closed, shut indoors
as caught fire reflects amber eyes, a shutter of light,

soft to touch. The moon doesn't listen, its blank-grey
face says, *I've always been close, always sniffed you out.*

She scents. Lets laundry pile up, collects must.
Pelt stripped and washed, teeth marks and rips –

she tastes blood, a hideous hunger. Night flash of cubs
murdered in a lack, by her own eye-teeth for no one else

to have them, she spites herself, howls unheard
at a forgotten pack. Will they know what she's done?

She licks her scars, paces rooms, wants the walls to hug
her, haunched in its corners, awake and unclothed

in the moon's light, writes names on her belly,
Anubis, Fenrir, Kerberos, keeps her den warm for them

in case they return. Her neck bristling, hair matted,
teeth worn, and still she calls to him, still fighting

the night. She calls to him to return to what she tore
apart in a burning house, to what might have been.

*Sumerian Dog Goddess of Fertility

The Escape

The trick was sewn into your mouth,
commissioned by a mirror. You complained
about Stockholm Syndrome as I handed you
means of getting free. You suspected
the tricks were faked. You wanted to fly
the plane, not just sit next to emergency exits.

Let me fly you to Uluru, land on sacred rock,
take in the landscape. We are always trying to escape.
You pour your heart out, always on the run.
Perhaps I'll be a wild man or a card-sharp on Coney Island.
How about a trip to the Bombay slums? You ask.
They don't call it that these days, I sigh.

Take these keys, take this knife, these pills, this ring,
these handcuffs. Take them
three times a day with meals, be a showman
at baffling us all until you're judged safe,
do the world tour. We cut out pictures
from *Conjurors Monthly. Put me in a straightjacket,*

you command quietly. How thrilling to be
so close to death. I lower you into packing crates,
boilers, wet sheets, machines, the belly of a whale.
I challenge you to escape from a beer barrel.
That's the hardest trick of all, you smile.
Write down the history of your magic, tell me

you're a liar and fraud and describe the torture,
overflowing with water. You turn into a bird
in front of me, spread your blue wings and sing
your song of a lifetime of escaping
behind curtains, you say - *watch*
and learn, We'll make these tricks into art.

The Angel

He wears a strong coat of wood pulp and bark.
A veneer, polished, shines when waxed. When bathed
and clean – in a certain light he shines
like a pigeon or a magpie glimmer.
He wears a long coat to hide behind –
he won't show his broken wings, his wounds like panic
and hell-flight are gripped tight over broken
bodies at night. He mutters and mumbles
in his sleep, so low I can barely hear.
He says prayers for the poor, the cracked and littered
under floorboards, spiders, the smell of mud
and police stations. For those lost behind
doors. Perhaps I passed him on the street once,
perhaps he thought it was me screaming like a cat
in darkness, but we both know it was him, alone,
made of the devil, holding on to a lifeboat made
of his body – covered in leaves and feathers.

The Thirst

The storm had not yet started, but it was close, a charged and sullied July heat
when he told me things had got out of hand,
things I couldn't take in, stuffed like a blister burst of insects, furrowed
deep in bones. He was wind blown inside
after a lifetime wandering half-awake from bus shelter to somewhere safe,
He threw up a million conundrums while I lived in humdrum,
using teapots, noticed cracked-pits, graphs and joined dots, offering cups of tea, washed his clothes,
offered strokes. *Come inside,*

sit down beside me, I lit incense to bless the house the way my aunt
showed me that summer when she came and prayed,
chanting every morning, filling the rooms with smoke and telling me how her
mother had hidden her in the Karnafuli, told her to breathe
through a small hollow reed, how to stay alive in the river during riots and mass murder.
He kept telling me things, things I didn't want to hear
but couldn't stop hearing, how the top of his head came loose and he saw God
dressed in sky – flying from an atom, *He had a quiff,*
and a moustache, I didn't know what he wanted. He told me a voice had appeared
in his head when he was dying of thirst, creased

and matted on the streets near the Angel, *get up, it told me, and keep walking.*
I was collapsed from exhaustion, but moved myself to a place
behind some bins behind a shop, and found a place, like an alcove, where I fell, found a water tap,
and I could drink. I lived there for days, he said.

We talked for hours in my kitchen as I breathed second hand smoke,
but it took me a long time to admit I saw them too –
all swarming around me from inside atoms, swimming into my face with surprised expressions, I
got the feeling they liked me.
Perhaps it's because we were like rescue dogs, neglected children, He wondered,
Leaves had really wrapped
and sprung from his hands, *and the white light, that was real too.*
He mused it might be his brain shutting down,
but that room I was in after I took the pills, the room with those people
and the strange blue bird, that was real.
Go back, go back they all kept saying. He was all fragments, *I talk in my sleep*
these days, sometimes I scream.
He told me life had smashed him, shrapnelled him through the mirror of his face.
I don't really understand how I'm alive,
he said. He kept talking to me in a slow low voice, strangled with gravel, and told me
he had a choir of angels in his head.

65

*And I hate angels and choral music. He was smiling. They wont leave me alone
and make me think I must be dead.*

I couldn't see what was inside him. We talked together all night, all day repairing
the last thirty years. *The kids we were no longer exist,*
I said, and we stood together – me not fully taking it in, this blessing of the world
around us. I was still sitting in that log cabin

on Quadra Island where the man covered in grass and leaves kept talking
to me in East Coast Salish, *Return our bones.*
He was so insistent, and I turned away, I told myself it was just my imagination,
and I felt the man follow me to the top
of Malahat mountain, where I danced for him, danced for their bones.
Perhaps it was just my imagination, perhaps I was lonely,
needing someone to share beauty and sorrow with, or needing to be needed,
to be important to someone, or something bigger then we can become.
I tasted God that afternoon, years ago, in June – sitting alone on a bench in Cornwall,
watching hikers catch their fingers in a locked gate.
I had the answer to the latch, but couldn't tell them, they hadn't asked me
for help. I sat crying, thinking of all the solutions the gods have for us,
and we never ask them, never even ask ourselves. I couldn't take it in,
all these bursts of compassion, tears while listening to prayers.

Return our bones ... Now in small hours as the storm breaks, caught in a wave of atoms,
a standing ovation of thunder, I stretch my arm out
of the kitchen window, hold out a glass
to collect drops obsessed with lightning. The sky's purple light
in a night current, and he says he has never seen a storm like it,
says it is right above my head, smiles, I offer him the water and we drink to the rain.

The Return

I arrived at your door, defeated, prodigal, dressed
in sheep's clothes, skin primed – made an effort that day.

    She saw the signs, a face changed with time,
    unable to see, what he'd become, what he'd done.

I had a book in my hand, ran to the bus driver,
panicked with second thought's, let me off at the next stop.

    She saw signs, songs he wrote on the old tape recorder,
    that one no one could understand. She couldn't listen.

I returned, pushed out of a tube that pumped me away,
pushed life back in through suction, charcoal and drip.

    She saw the signs, but never spoke their names, fed him
    all she had, shopping channels, diet food, pushed back in.

I told them, no – don't do this, don't want this, and they left.
I faced the final push, cried out – like a child – for help.

    She saw the signs, animal signs, pale gums, moist eyes,
    vital signs, pulse, she prayed – keep his body alive.

I wanted to be someone else, wasted trials of life, time to cry
wolf-shaped boy, hung for a lamb in grandmother's house.

    She howled for him in her belly, an oblivion space, cut
    with canines, a tear of first born, what big teeth he had.

I amassed so many scars, they held me in place, my timber,
grey, one good eye, aged legs limped towards her.

Reunion

We remembered together, the miners' strike,
we shared the past through those Thatcher times,
donkey jackets, bleakness of shut, staring
slag heaps, shouting from picket lines.

We laughed in our conspiracy of closeness
that faded like tapestry. I was talking about the end
of secured tenancies in 1989, he was shouting
things about socialism from the next room.

Then we fell to talking about guilt, and tripped
into an awkward corner of sunlit shame,
and we were silent, thinking of love, but couldn't say
the names of the ones that hurt us.

We distracted ourselves, he – by muttering
and rolling cigarettes, stroking the edge of his can
of beer, and me by staring into space and
writing everything down.

Burning Tower

You, creased, crumpled like the newspaper
caught in that blaze. I, shattered, as we sat in silence,
watching the newsflash, and you said, *perhaps*
we should talk about the headlines, pretend
that we're the burning tower.

All I thought was how their washing machines
and fridges exploded – and their children died.
I wanted to tell you how everything just boiled
down to finding a way to say *can you see all my new*
improved features or am I the girl you still remember?

I could rescue you from a cooled inferno,
lit by the shine of the kitchen's chandelier, its glass
scattering shadows across our faces,
and you warn me as you roll a cigarette on the table
that some souls are born inside a house on fire.

Babel

When she first started speaking he said,
Go on, I'm listening,
She saw his eyes were the moon and stars,
his lips the night sky.
She forced gusts out of her lips, out in spurts
as he kept on and on and on
pacing the floor, waving his hands. She sputtered
some babble out as he tried
to follow her all over the house. *I'm in crevices,*
under floorboards, behind the fridge,
she muttered. He tried to quiet his mind in waves,
Poor little girl, he said, *I always knew*
you talked nonsense as she repeated *slow down,*
slow down, slow down.

Shell Shock

I listen to heating pipes and your cough,
ask you to play something quiet and close
the window. You point to the moon, frost-bitten
in daylight, tell me you're scared of the stories

you were told, about falling from bridges,
being too beautiful, too clever, too bold.
I can't help shouting at you, *it's OK to be quiet,
to sleep, to live, to grow old.* You say we're similar

because you're the sound of jet engines,
I'm the sound of thunder. Your smoke trails
out of the window. I can hear the roar of a fierce,
hollow purpose in your head explode.

You said you were built of a lifetime of stories,
slotted back into a shape of a man. Nothing's
the same when you came back. Stories of blood,
your grandfather's dying cough. *Tell me,*

are you sure? By the kitchen table, you smile
in Morse code, *your face's haunted, where did you go?*
You wash my dishes with heartbreak, find music
pacing the floor, *are you sure you heard them right,*

your grandfather's secrets? ... you become a mirage
in the kitchen. You say you like the cold.
I don't know, nothing makes sense. I'm getting old.
You tell me his last words were, *This wallpaper's got to go.*

The room smells of saltpetre, shared love songs.
We hold hands, wait for the bomb to drop,
stranded in a kitchen, avoiding shrapnel,
history, housework, heartache and fall-out.

Time Minus

She wants to be told once more how she was loved,
and in hunger he spews out the contents of the years,
working backwards, without a gravity to hold him.
He doesn't understand how he got from place to place,
no choices, poor choices, sins of omission.
She sees it clearly, it was all buttons, *press here* written
everywhere. He was looking for the emergency stop,
but was tied up in velocity and zero gravity and love.
Newton's third law, equal and opposite.
She smiles at his unstoppable force and her inertia.
You need to contain your own rocket fuel and thrusters,
she tries to explain, not really understanding anything,
just accepting the laws of physics. He's got nothing
to complain about, a vacuum packed series of probabilities
and trying to understand how space works.
It just does, she says.
She makes lunch, talking about her choices and her animal
brain that went on for too long, and thought too hard
about what love really was, and missed it.
I wanted to know how it works she told him, and I just
don't understand. He holds her hand.
*It's time to leave the past behind, and trust
in your own velocity. Love just does the work,* he says.

Practical Physics

Night Sky's all charged up, her clusters
of moles and scars – where she churns up
stars excite the nebula of nipples
and makes them hard. Her body is capped silken
as she charts down radio waves.
I can see you with my milky eyes – and I'll lick you
like a mother dog. She's husky to her Einstein,
as they grow old together side by side.
In bed they read the Vedas together.
After they make love, they sip chocolate
and rum. Einstein, suddenly shy, looks coy
from his beard, where he wipes the fluids
and chemicals they've intimately shared.
I hardly know you, he declares. Night Sky touches
him under dark blankets, feels his full moon.
As he gives the all clear, they fly again,
rapture through Pleiades, over Aldebaran,
The Great Bear. When the weather's good,
I can see them from Beachy Head.

Flood

Inside this cage lives a wave,
shaped like a man,

singing inside a box –
the smallest I have ever seen.

I peer through bars, into the box
where tears seep through,

Just let him out! I call
to the attendant, no one comes,

and I wonder off, into the trees
to think about

how I am a wave,
and where I should crash,

I hear the music,
so loud I want to stop my ears,

a roar of surf.
When I return,

The cage, broken, the box
– carried away,

and the surrounding flood,
sounds magnificent.

Acknowledgements

Thanks to the editors of the following publications where versions of these poems have appeared: *Obsessed with Pipework, Moth, Ink Sweat and Tears, Tears in the Fence, The Interpreter's House, Gold Dust, Lampeter Review, Paper Swans, Templar, Antiphon, Poetry Salzburg Review, Poetry Shed, Ebracce, Elbow Room, Clear Poetry, Agenda* and Paper Swans Press *The Chronicles of Eve*. Thanks to Maria C. McCarthy and Bob Carling for their patience and help with editing this collection.

Some of these poems appear in the pamphlets: *The Swell* (2016), published by Telltale Press, and *Joyride* (2017), published by Black Light Engine Room Press.

Thanks to Susan Wicks, Sarah Salway, Gillian Clarke, Abegail Morley, Mimi Khalvati, Patricia McCarthy and David Caddy for help and advice. Thanks to my poetry community for their support and encouragement, to all my friends and family for cheering me on. Thanks Simon Tje Jones for your friendship and inspiration.

Cultured Llama Publishing
Poems | Stories | Curious Things

Cultured Llama was born in a converted stable. This creature of humble birth drank greedily from the creative source of the poets, writers, artists and musicians that visited, and soon the llama fulfilled the destiny of its given name.

Cultured Llama aspires to quality from the first creative thought through to the finished product.

www.culturedllama.co.uk

Also published by Cultured Llama

Poetry

strange fruits by Maria C. McCarthy
Paperback; 72pp; 203×127mm; 978-0-9568921-0-2; July 2011

A Radiance by Bethany W. Pope
Paperback; 72pp; 203×127mm; 978-0-9568921-3-3; June 2012

The Night My Sister Went to Hollywood by Hilda Sheehan
Paperback; 82pp; 203×127mm; 978-0-9568921-8-8; March 2013

Notes from a Bright Field by Rose Cook
Paperback; 104pp; 203×127mm; 978-0-9568921-9-5; July 2013

The Fire in Me Now by Michael Curtis
Paperback; 90pp; 203×127mm; 978-0-9926485-4-1; August 2014

Cold Light of Morning by Julian Colton
Paperback; 90pp; 203×127mm; 978-0-9926485-7-2; March 2015

Zygote Poems by Richard Thomas
Paperback; 66pp; 178×127mm; 978-0-9932119-5-9; July 2015

Les Animots: A Human Bestiary by Gordon Meade, images by Douglas Robertson
Hardback; 166pp; 203×127mm; 70 line illus.; 978-0-9926485-9-6; December 2015

Memorandum: Poems for the Fallen by Vanessa Gebbie
Paperback; 90pp; 203×127mm; 978-0-9932119-4-2; February 2016

The Light Box by Rosie Jackson
Paperback; 108pp; 203×127mm; 978-0-9932119-7-3; March 2016

There Are No Foreign Lands by Mark Holihan
Paperback; 96pp; 203×127mm; 978-0-9932119-8-0; June 2016

After Hours by David Cooke
Paperback; 92pp; 203×127mm; 978-0-9957381-0-2; April 2017

There Are Boats on the Orchard by Maria C. McCarthy
Paperback; 36pp; 210×115mm; SKU: 001; July 2017

Hearth by Rose Cook
Paperback; 120pp; 203×127mm; 978-0-9957381-4-0; September 2017

The Year of the Crab by Gordon Meade
Paperback; 88pp; 203×127mm; 978-0-9957381-3-3; October 2017

Short stories

Canterbury Tales on a Cockcrow Morning by Maggie Harris
Paperback; 138pp; 203×127mm; 978-0-9568921-6-4; September 2012

As Long as it Takes by Maria C. McCarthy
Paperback; 168pp; 203×127mm; 978-0-9926485-1-0; February 2014

In Margate by Lunchtime by Maggie Harris
Paperback; 204pp; 203×127mm; 978-0-9926485-3-4; February 2015

The Lost of Syros by Emma Timpany
Paperback; 128pp; 203×127mm; 978-0-9932119-2-8; July 2015

Only the Visible Can Vanish by Anna Maconochie
Paperback; 158pp; 203×127mm; 978-0-9932119-9-7; September 2016

Who Killed Emil Kreisler? by Nigel Jarrett
Paperback; 208pp; 203×127mm; 978-0-9568921-1-9; November 2016

A Short History of Synchronised Breathing and other stories by Vanessa Gebbie
Paperback; 132pp; 203×127mm; 978-0-9568921-2-6; February 2017

In the Wild Wood by Frances Gapper
Paperback; 212pp; 203×127mm; 978-0-9957381-6-4; June 2017

A Witness of Waxwings by Alison Lock
Paperback; 128pp; 203×127mm; 978-0-9957381-5-7; December 2017

Dip Flash by Jonathan Pinnock
Paperback; 154pp; 203×127mm; 978-0-9957381-7-1; March 2018

Curious things

Digging Up Paradise: Potatoes, People and Poetry in the Garden of England by Sarah Salway
Paperback; 164pp; 203×203mm; 76 colour illus.; 978-0-9926485-6-5; June 2014

Punk Rock People Management: A No-Nonsense Guide to Hiring, Inspiring and Firing Staff by Peter Cook
Paperback; 40pp; 210×148mm; 978-0-9932119-0-4; February 2015

Do it Yourself: A History of Music in Medway by Stephen H. Morris
Paperback; 504pp; 229×152mm; 978-0-9926485-2-7; April 2015

The Music of Business: Business Excellence Fused with Music by Peter Cook
Paperback; 318pp; 210×148mm; 978-0-9932119-1-1; May 2015

The Hungry Writer by Lynne Rees
Paperback; 246pp; 244×170mm; 57 colour illus.; 978-0-9932119-3-5; September 2015

Solid Mental Grace: Listening to the Music of Yes by Simon Barrow
Paperback; 232pp; 210×148mm; 978-0-9957381-8-8; March 2018

96a Henwood Green
Road, Pembury
TN2 4LN.

Lightning Source UK Ltd.
Milton Keynes UK
UKHW03f1450190418
321342UK00001B/76/P

9 780995 738119